OUR
GREAT
STATES

WHAT'S GREAT ABOUT

RHODE ISLAND?

✳ Rebecca Felix

LERNER PUBLICATIONS ✳ MINNEAPOLIS

CONTENTS

Copyright © 2015
by Lerner Publishing Group, Inc.

Content Consultant: Erik Christiansen,
Professor of History, Rhode Island College

Lerner Publications Company
A division of Lerner Publishing Group, Inc.
241 First Avenue North
Minneapolis, MN 55401 USA

For reading levels and more information, look
up this title at www.lernerbooks.com.

Main body text set in ITC Franklin Gothic Std
Book Condensed 12/15.
Typeface provided by Adobe Systems.

Library of Congress Cataloging-in-Publication
Data

Felix, Rebecca, 1984–
        What's great about Rhode Island? / by
Rebecca Felix.
            pages   cm. — (Our great states)
        Includes index.
        Audience: Ages 7–11.
        ISBN 978-1-4677-3856-9 (lib. bdg. :
alk. paper) — ISBN 978-1-4677-6080-5
(pbk.) — 978-1-4677-6258-8 (EB pdf)
        1. Oregon--Juvenile literature. I. Title.
F79.3.F47 2015
974.5—dc23   2014029146

Manufactured in the United States of America
1 - PC – 12/31/14

RHODE ISLAND Welcomes You!

There's tons to see and do in the smallest state in the nation! Rhode Island is only 48 miles (77 kilometers) long and 37 miles (60 km) wide. Rhode Island is nicknamed the Ocean State. It has more than one hundred beaches. Many Rhode Islanders swim and boat. Offshore, yachts and sailboats bob in the Atlantic Ocean. Fishers catch lobsters and large clams. Narragansett Bay runs up the eastern part of the state. Many people live along the bay in busy coastal cities. Outside these bustling cities is the rural western half of Rhode Island. The state's short borders are full of natural beauty and fun activities. Read on to learn all about ten things that make Rhode Island great!

MASSACHUSETTS

CONNECTICUT

Woonsocket

Cumberland

Blackstone River

Jerimoth Hill
(812 feet/
247 m)

North
Providence

Pawtucket

Providence

East Providence

Scituate
Reservoir

Cranston

Pawtuxet River

West Warwick

Warwick

Coventry

Narragansett Bay

Sakonnet River

Wood River

N

Newport

Pawcatuck River

RHODE ISLAND SOUND

Miles
0   5   10

0   5   10   15
Kilometers

ATLANTIC OCEAN

Block
Island

Explore Rhode Island's
beaches and all the places in
between. Just turn the page
to find out all about
the OCEAN STATE. >

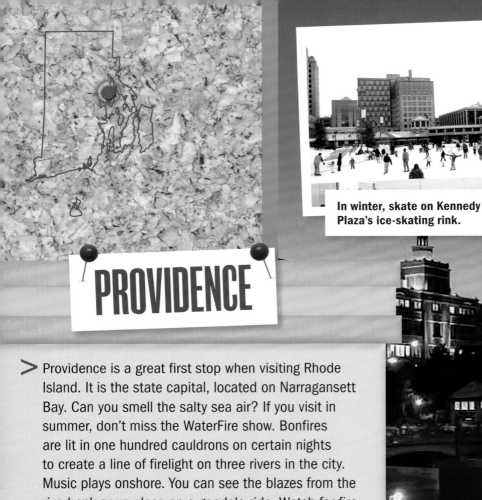

In winter, skate on Kennedy Plaza's ice-skating rink.

PROVIDENCE

> Providence is a great first stop when visiting Rhode Island. It is the state capital, located on Narragansett Bay. Can you smell the salty sea air? If you visit in summer, don't miss the WaterFire show. Bonfires are lit in one hundred cauldrons on certain nights to create a line of firelight on three rivers in the city. Music plays onshore. You can see the blazes from the riverbank or up close on a gondola ride. Watch for fire jugglers and dancers!

During the day, the Providence Children's Museum is a good spot to visit. Climb the museum's two-story maze. Create art and conduct science experiments at the Discovery Studio. A group of life-sized, alien puppets sometimes visit here! In summer, gather for a picnic at Kennedy Plaza's Burnside Park. Listen to live music or outdoor story time. In winter, whiz and twirl around the plaza's ice-skating rink. It is nearly the size of a football field!

Wave hello to the dragon as you walk into the Providence Children's Museum.

ROGER WILLIAMS PARK

> Imagine a park where you can paddleboat on ponds, examine fossils, and see exotic animals. You just pictured Roger Williams Park. It is only minutes from Providence. More than 100 acres (40 hectares) of the park's 435 total acres (176 hectares) are ponds. Rent a paddleboat shaped like a giant swan. Or take a duck boat tour to explore the ponds. The duck boat can drive on land and float in water!

Crocodiles, camels, and other animals roam the Roger Williams Park Zoo. Walk along the zoo's paths to view them. Then stop at the carousel for a ride. Get ready for more fun! The Museum of Natural History and Planetarium is also in the park. Thousands of fossils from around the world are housed here. The planetarium is a huge dome that shows twinkling stars. It has special programs about the moon, astronauts, and space.

Explore Roger Williams Park's ponds in a swan paddleboat.

ROGER WILLIAMS

Roger Williams was a religious leader. He lived in Massachusetts in the 1600s. Some people did not like his religious ideas. In 1636, Williams was banned from the state. He traveled to what is now Providence. He bought land from American Indians and founded the city. Then he created the colony of Rhode Island. He decided people there should have complete freedom to choose their religion.

9

EASTON'S BEACH

> Rhode Island has many beaches. But there's only one where you can skateboard, learn to sail, and compete in a singing competition! Easton's Beach is the only ocean beach open to everyone in Newport. It has an outdoor skateboard park, playground, and snack bar. An aquarium borders the beach. It holds small sharks, lobsters, and octopuses.

On the beach, people swim and build sandcastles. Newport is known as the sailing capital of the world. Can you spot many sailboats offshore? If you are seven or older and pass a swimming test, you can take a sailing class at Fort Adams Sailing Association near Easton's Beach! Learn to set sails and right a capsized boat. You'll also learn sailing lingo. Ahoy!

Easton's Beach stays busy after sunset in summer. Each Thursday night is the Easton's Beach Idol contest. It's a singing competition based on the show *American Idol*. See if you can outsing other kids on the beach. The winner receives a free T-shirt and two free hours of studio recording time! Afterward, sit in the sand and listen to storytellers or watch seaside magicians perform.

Learn to sail at Fort Adams Sailing Association near Easton's Beach.

Play at Easton's Beach on a rented bodyboard.

Decorate gingerbread and sugar cookies at the Children's Fair.

NEWPORT WINTER FESTIVAL

> The Newport Winter Festival is held each February. There are many fun things to see and do at the festival. Start your celebration by joining a giant outdoor pillow fight. Then watch ice shavings fly as artists carve ice blocks into statues. Artists sculpt the blocks using chain saws, blow-dryers, and sanders. If ice isn't your thing, create your own sand sculpture at the festival. Sand sculpture contests are held at Easton's Beach. All ages are allowed to enter. There is also horseback riding on the beach. Bring a coat! Rhode Island's beaches are chilly in winter.

Stay bundled up to go ice-skating or watch the figure-skating show. Then warm up inside while decorating cookies or making marshmallow snowmen. Many kinds of crafts, plus games and music, are at the festival's Children's Fair. End your tour with a party. A local dance team hosts a dance party on several of the festival nights. It is for kids only, and the team teaches all the coolest new moves.

RHODE ISLAND WINTERS

Rhode Island gets snow in winter. Most of it falls in February. But the snow doesn't often stay on the ground for very long before melting. The state can also be hit by winter Nor'easters. These are wicked, windy blizzards. They bring wet snow and ice to the East Coast. The storms can cause coastal areas to flood.

PAWSOX GAME

> Have you ever stood on the pitcher's mound at a baseball game? Get your chance at a Pawtucket Red Sox game! The Pawtucket Red Sox are a minor-league baseball team. They are often called the PawSox. Their home stadium is McCoy Stadium in Pawtucket. PawSox games are tons of fun. Some games have themes, such as *Star Wars* or Halloween. On these days, come dressed up in your favorite costumes. Peanuts, popcorn, and hot dogs are only one dollar each on Mondays!

Become a Kids Club member by signing up online. Members can volunteer to kick off special Friday-night games. If your name is chosen, you will stand at a microphone on the field. The crowd and players will all turn to you. Then you'll yell "Play ball!" to begin the game. Some games end with fireworks above the field. And on one special night each year, a slumber party caps off the game! Families can sign up to sleep right on the field under the stars.

Meet Sox, a PawSox mascot, at McCoy Stadium.

Enjoy popcorn for just one dollar if you make it to a Monday PawSox game.

SOUTH COUNTY BALLOON FESTIVAL

> Look up in Kingston! If you're here in summer, you might see hot air balloons floating in the sky. The South County Balloon Festival is held each July. Up to fourteen aeronauts bring balloons to the three-day festival. Watch these balloons inflate with hot air. If the weather isn't too windy, climb into the basket and take a ride! The balloons lift you up. But they are attached to the ground with ropes. This way, riders don't float away from the festival.

If the weather is too windy for balloon rides, watch a kite team fly enormous kites. Did you see the flying woman as you looked to the sky? A cannon lady rockets from a cannon barrel several times a day. Other performances include log rolling and a wild animal show. Keep busy until dark at the festival fishing pond and rock-climbing wall. When the sun sets, look to the sky again. The balloons are lit like lanterns. On Saturday, fireworks light up the sky after this balloon release.

Take a ride in a hot air balloon basket at the South County Balloon Festival (*right*). See if you can make it to the top of the rock-climbing wall at the festival (*left*).

BLOCK ISLAND

> There are many small islands off Rhode Island's coast. But there is only one where you can pet a llama and explore on horseback. Board a ferry and head to Block Island! The island has many beaches. Do you want to touch a crab? Do so safely at the Block Island Maritime Institute. It has a program called Creature Feature. Visitors can touch crabs, sea urchins, or lobsters in special tanks. Get an up-close look at plankton under a microscope.

After learning about Block Island's creatures, explore the island itself. Rent a kayak and check out the island's waters. On land, visit Rustic Rides Farm and go horseback riding. Find other hooved animals at the island petting zoo. There are many animals here you'd never expect to see! Black swans, red kangaroos, and lemurs all live here. You can even get nose to nose with a camel.

Search for sand dollars on the beaches of Block Island.

Pet a zedonk, a cross between a donkey and a zebra, at Rustic Rides Farm.

COGGESHALL FARM
MUSEUM

> The Coggeshall Farm Museum is a farm from the past. This museum in Bristol gives visitors a look at how people lived in Rhode Island after the Revolutionary War (1775–1783). Coggeshall Farm workers plant and pick from the gardens. They chop firewood and care for livestock. All the workers are dressed in historic costumes. When you visit, be ready to jump in and help! Visitors can help with all farm activities.

The museum holds special events each season. One event is Breakfast in the Barnyard. For this, get to the farm early—before the animals are even awake! Milk the cows, gather eggs from the chickens, and help brush the horses. Then it's time for breakfast. Visitors use a cookbook from the 1700s to make johnnycakes, a kind of pancake. In spring, watch the sheep get haircuts at the sheep-shearing festival. Autumn is harvest-time at the farm. It's celebrated with a yearly fair. Take part in a watermelon seed-spitting contest, games, and music.

US CONSTITUTION

During the Revolutionary War, the thirteen American colonies fought for independence from Great Britain. Rhode Island was one of these colonies. On May 4, 1776, it was the first colony to declare its independence. After the war, all thirteen colonies created the US Constitution. It had laws for the new country. Rhode Island initially voted against it. The state finally signed the document in 1790.

Learn how to make johnnycakes at the Coggeshall Farm Museum.

NARRAGANSETT BAY

> Narragansett Bay is an inlet of the Atlantic Ocean. Winter is a special time here. The bay becomes home to hundreds of seals. Bundle up and board an open-air boat for a seal tour! Save the Bay Seal Watch Cruises leave from Newport and Westerly. The boat splashes past small, rocky islands. Listen to your guide talk about the different seals in the bay. You're most likely to see harbor seals on the tour. But hooded seals and harp seals swim there too.

Rose Island is a popular place to spot harbor seals. Some Save the Bay tour boats let passengers get out to explore Rose Island. The Rose Island Lighthouse Foundation offers a similar tour. You can visit the island lighthouse. View furniture, photos, and information about families that lived and worked in the lighthouse more than one hundred years ago.

Tour the Rose Island Lighthouse, which was built in the 1800s.

HARBOR SEAL MIGRATION

Harbor seals live in the waters near Maine and Canada most of the year. In winter, they migrate south to Narragansett Bay. The Atlantic Ocean gets very cold near Maine and Canada in winter. The waters in Narragansett Bay are a bit warmer. The seals feed on other marine life, such as squid and even lobsters.

WASHINGTON COUNTY FAIR

> The Washington County Fair takes place in the town of Richmond. The event celebrates Rhode Island's agriculture. The fair lasts five days each August. Enjoy rides, exhibits, concerts, and fireworks. Take part in one of the many competitions for kids. Carefully catch and throw an egg in an egg toss. Tie your leg to a partner's leg. Then hobble through a three-legged race! See how long you can stand up on stilts.

Next, show off your farming skills. If you've never milked an animal before, you can sign up for a milking contest. There's also a mooing contest. The final cow competition gets a little messy. It's a dung-throwing contest. Judges hand you a piece of dried cow poop. Fling it as far as you can! Then make sure you wash your hands, even though you can't use them in the next event. It is a mini blueberry–pie eating contest! Hold your hands behind your back. Then chew to be the first to finish your pie!

Grab a friend and enter the three-legged race at the Washington County Fair (*left*). Watch fireworks light up the night sky after a fun day at the fair (*below*).

YOUR TOP TEN!

You just read about ten things that make Rhode Island great. What would your Rhode Island top ten list include? What would you like to see? Write down your top ten choices on a separate sheet of paper. You can turn them into a book just like this one. Draw your own pictures. Or add pictures from the Internet or magazines. Have fun planning your Rhode Island trip!

RHODE ISLAND BY MAP

> ## MAP KEY

⭐ Capital city

◯ City

◎ Point of interest

▲ Highest elevation

—·— State border

Visit www.lerneresource.com to learn more about the state flag of Rhode Island.

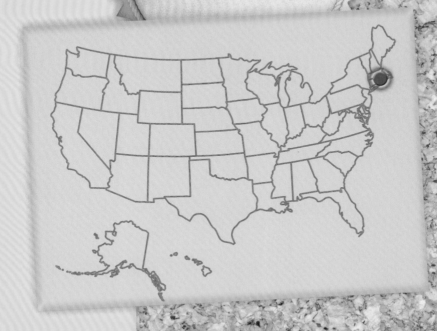

Woonsocket

Blackstone River

Cumberland

McCoy Stadium

Providence Children's Museum

WaterFire

Roger Williams Park

Museum of Natural History and Planetarium

Pawtucket

North Providence

▲ Jerimoth Hill (812 feet/ 247 m)

Providence

East Providence

Cranston

Scituate Reservoir

Pawtuxet River

West Warwick

Warwick

Coggeshall Farm Museum (Bristol)

Coventry

Narragansett Bay

Sakonnet River

Wood River

N

South County Balloon Festival (Kingston)

Newport

Washington County Fair (Richmond)

Newport Winter Festival

Easton's Beach

Save the Bay Seal Watch Cruises

Pawcatuck River

RHODE ISLAND SOUND

Miles

0   5   10

0   5   10   15

Kilometers

Block Island Maritime Institute

Block Island

ATLANTIC OCEAN

RHODE ISLAND FACTS

NICKNAME: The Ocean State

SONG: "Rhode Island's It for Me" by Charlie Hall and Maria Day

MOTTO: "Hope"

FLOWER: common blue violet

> **TREE:** red maple

FISH: striped bass

> **BIRD:** Rhode Island Red chicken

FOOD: greening apple

DATE AND RANK OF STATEHOOD: May 29, 1790; the 13th state

> **CAPITAL:** Providence

AREA: 1,221 square miles (3,162 sq. km)

AVERAGE JANUARY TEMPERATURE: 29°F (−2°C)

AVERAGE JULY TEMPERATURE: 71°F (22°C)

POPULATION AND RANK: 1,051,511; 43rd (2013)

MAJOR CITIES AND POPULATIONS: Providence (177,994), Warwick (81,971), Cranston (80,566), Pawtucket (71,172), East Providence (47,149)

NUMBER OF US CONGRESS MEMBERS: 2 representatives; 2 senators

NUMBER OF ELECTORAL VOTES: 4

NATURAL RESOURCES: minerals, soil, fish

> **AGRICULTURAL PRODUCTS:** sod, ornamental trees and shrubs, milk, hay, potatoes

MANUFACTURED GOODS: pharmaceuticals and chemicals, jewelry, silverware, metal products

STATE HOLIDAYS AND CELEBRATIONS: Rhode Island Independence Day

GLOSSARY

aeronaut: a person who controls a hot air balloon

agriculture: the raising of crops and animals

banned: officially kept from something

capsized: turned over in water

cauldron: a big metal pot

exotic: unusual and from a country that is far away

gondola: a long, light boat with a flat bottom

independence: being free from another country's control

inlet: a narrow body of water that cuts into land from a bigger body of water

lingo: special words or language used for a certain activity

migrate: to move to another place

minor league: the league below Major League Baseball that helps players prepare to play professionally

plankton: tiny plants and animals that float in oceans and lakes

US Constitution: the written document that explains how the US government works

LERNER

SOURCE

Expand learning beyond the printed book. Download free, complementary educational resources for this book from our website, www.lerneresource.com.

FURTHER INFORMATION

Cunningham, Kevin. *The Rhode Island Colony*. New York: Children's Press, 2012. Learn about the creation of the United States from thirteen original colonies, which included Rhode Island.

Family Days Out: Rhode Island
http://www.familydaysout.com/kids-things-to-do-usa/rhodeisland
Find a list of all kinds of fun activities, sorted by type and age, to do in Rhode Island.

Friesen, Helen Lepp. *The Ocean State: Rhode Island*. New York: AV2 by Weigl, 2013. Read about Rhode Island's history, people, culture, and geography.

Little Rhodies Kids Zone
http://sos.ri.gov/kidszone
Find games, coloring pages, and cartoons that share tons of information about Rhode Island's government and state history.

PawSox: Kids Corner
http://www.milb.com/content/page.jsp?sid=t533&ymd=20100313&content_id=8775862&vkey=team4
Sign up to become a Kids Club Member of the PawSox baseball team, print out fun activities, and register for special events.

Ransom, Candice. *Who Wrote the U.S. Constitution? And Other Questions about the Constitutional Convention of 1787*. Minneapolis: Lerner Publications, 2011. Learn more about the writing of the US Constitution.

INDEX

PHOTO ACKNOWLEDGMENTS

The images in this book are used with the permission of: © Shutterstock Images, pp. 1, 11 (top), 15 (bottom), 16–17, 24–25; NASA, pp. 2–3; © Spirit of America/Shutterstock Images, p. 4; © Marianne Campolongo/Shutterstock Images, pp. 4–5; © Laura Westlund/Independent Picture Service, pp. 5, 27; © Joy Brown/Shutterstock Images, p. 6; WFProvidence, pp. 6–7; © Franck Fotos/Alamy, p. 7; © Norman Eggert/Alamy, pp. 8–9; © Art Fleury/Alamy, p. 9 (top); Library of Congress, p. 9 (bottom) (LC-DIG-det-4a12208); © Robert Francis/Robert Harding/Newscom, pp. 10–11; © Fuse/Thinkstock, p. 11 (bottom); © pilipphoto/Shutterstock Images, p. 12; © aphotostory/Shutterstock Images, pp. 12–13; © Triff/Shutterstock Images, p. 13; Public Domain, pp. 14–15; Paul Keleher, p. 15 (top); © Thinkstock, pp. 17 (left), 29 (top right), 29 (bottom left), 29 (bottom right); © Chatchai Somwat/Shutterstock Images, p. 17 (right); © Arena Creative/Shutterstock Images, pp. 18–19; © Julie Deshaies/Shutterstock Images, p. 19 (top); © Nic Hamilton Photographic/Alamy, p. 19 (bottom); © Mark Hayes/Shutterstock Images, p. 20; Flickr, pp. 20–21; © Phil Degginger/Alamy, p. 21; © Mary Terriberry/Shutterstock Images, pp. 22–23; © Allan Wood Photography/Shutterstock Images, p. 23 (top); © Ken Wolter/Shutterstock Images, p. 23 (bottom); © ERproductions Ltd/Thinkstock, p. 25 (left); © A.B.G./Shutterstock Images, p. 25 (right); © nicoolay'iStockphoto, p. 26; © Holly Kuchera/Shutterstock Images, p. 29 (top left).

Cover: © Alwoodphoto/Dreamstime.com (lighthouse); © John Fuller/Shutterstock.com (seals) © Stephen Wood (carnival); © iStockphoto.com/DenisTangneyJr., (Providence); © Laura Westlund/Independent Picture Service (map); © iStockphoto.com/fpm (seal); © iStockphoto.com/vicm (pushpins); © iStockphoto.com/benz190 (cork board).